Leave No MilSpouse Behind

Inspiring Stories That Empower Dreams

Michelle A. Faust & Laura Briggs

Featuring:
Sara Copp, Sienna Newton Dohse, Krystalore Crews
&
Betsy Moore Nelson

Copyright © 2024 by Michelle Faust
All rights reserved.

No part of this book may be reproduced or transmitted in any form or by any means, electronic or mechanical, including photocopying, recording, or by any information storage and retrieval system, without permission in writing from the copyright owner.

ISBN Paperback: 979-8-8693-5839-4
ISBN eBook: 979-8-8693-5840-0

Contents

Introduction 5

Chapter One: Reconsidering Your Career as a Military Spouse- Laura Briggs 8

The Pivot 8

Challenges Facing Military SpousesMoving Frequently 10

Licensing and certification concerns 12

Taking time off of work 13

How to support other military spouses in their careers 16

Share your story 17

Volunteer with organizations that support mil spouse efforts 17

Starting internship, mentoring, or job shadow opportunities 18

Help Spouses 1:1 18

Chapter Two: Be A Hawk- Betsy Moore Nelson 20

Those pesky quotes 26

Some of my truisms 30

Dual-Agency in the Military Family 33

Dealing with a spouse with Moral Injury 35

Be A Hawk! 36

Conclusion 36

Chapter Three: A Spouse Is A Spouse- Sara Copp 38

Chapter Four: Unleash Your Inner Warrior Within 51

Crews Beyond Limits Journal Prompts: 55

Chapter Five: Don't Be A Dependa- Sienna Newton Dohse 56

Chapter Six: Transition To Transformation-Michelle Faust 74

Introduction

My vision darted around, and I looked up to the second floor of the hotel atrium. I focused on a room that I could see filling with women. Looking at my phone, I picked up my pace to find the escalator. With a feeling of relief, I felt myself ascend to the second floor, and it was only a few quick steps away. I slowed my pace so as not to look at how I felt on the inside: a little frantic and unsure of coming.

On this day, I had a few places I could choose to be; at this conference, my husband was running a table, and this event hosted several inspiring and informational events.

Scanning the room, I chose a location near the front where some women had gathered. I had never met the women in this room before, but we all had one thing in common: we were military spouses.

The woman I sat by was as shy and reserved as I am. I asked her, "How was your day today?" She responded, "I am having a great day, and I am excited to hear from the speakers who were to encourage us today." I agreed with her, and we began to share our experiences over the past day and what we were looking forward to.

The two of us quickly became a group of eight, one of ten groups in the room. Lively chatter, and laughter quickly became a hushed silence as it was time for the speaker to take her place. I spent that day absorbed and lost in inspirational stories and narratives crafted to help and encourage every military spouse in the room. These women who spoke had overcome much, bearing battle scars that produced businesses, organizations, and a drive to make a difference.

The afternoon flew by; I gathered up the various papers collected during the day and knew it was time for me to go. I had mixed feelings as I walked out and stepped on the escalator. On the one hand, I was encouraged and inspired. On the other, I wished I could have a chance to sit down with the speakers over a cup of coffee and hear more of their stories. Within every crafted message is hidden a treasure trove of things that were not shared. Things of value that, for the sake of brevity and clarity, are left unsaid.

Conference speakers and successful people are nearly impossible to get time with. Schedules and demands make any prospect of a conversation to get past the crafted story possible. I wanted to connect with military spouses who had inspiring stories that empowered dreams; I found five powerful women. Women who are driven, gifted, and have wisdom. Women who fully represent what it means to be a military spouse and have a passion to leave no milspouse behind.

These five other women and I have come together to encourage, inspire, and raise awareness of what it is like to be a military spouse. We represent six different perspectives, all from different branches of service and backgrounds. We may be different, but we unify on one thing: We are military spouses, and we all have a passion for telling our stories.

These stories are to encourage, help, and provide guidance to other military spouses who may feel alone in what they are going through. When the idea came to me about authoring this collaboration, I had one fact that drove me to do it. When I would talk to military spouses, I kept hearing the same stories over and over again. Each person believed they were struggling alone in a battle that no one would understand; they did not realize they were joined in the same battle by many.

Silence does not mean a problem does not exist; it just means no one is talking. This book is intended to break the silence, open a dialogue, and let people know they are not alone. We are a community united on one fact: we are military spouses.

Together, we stand strong; together, we can be the people who choose to leave no milspouse behind.

Chapter One

Reconsidering Your Career as a Military Spouse-Laura Briggs

As a military spouse, you face unique challenges that call on you to ask questions about your career. The stress, schedule, and expectations of the military lifestyle often leave military spouses struggling to figure out how to start, continue, or grow their own careers.

When I met my husband, John, I was in the last year of my master's program. I planned to enter a Ph.D. program and had already been accepted. Thankfully, when he was transferred from WV to the DC area, my school had another campus in DC, so I could move my admission there. At the time, I had no idea what life moving as a military couple would look like. I knew it would involve moving to different locations, but I totally had to reconsider my own career. That was 15 years ago, and since then, I've dedicated a lot of my professional career to helping other military spouses find and grow meaningful mobile careers.

The Pivot

When I met my now husband, my educational and professional plan at the time was to finish my doctorate and become a professor. I'd never planned to spend my life with someone in the military, but I knew John was the one.

While I worked on my graduate classes at night, I taught in Baltimore City during the day. I figured it would help me to have a teaching credential in Maryland so that I could take that with me if we had to move out of the region in the future. Unfortunately, I quickly discovered that teaching wasn't for me, and I resigned my position the next year. I felt like a failure on a few fronts because I'd planned to go into education no matter what, and now that I'd had some on-the-job experience, I knew it wasn't right for me. So, what could I do to find or create a career that would move with us?

I was offered a job at a company I used to work with when I quit teaching in the marketing department, and I took it while I figured out what I wanted to do with my career. At that time, I was inspired to search for how to become a freelance writer since I'd always been interested in writing. I started a side hustle as a freelance writer, and this bloomed into a career that followed me as we moved to North Carolina, Indiana, Minnesota, and then Illinois for my husband's career.

My story is not unique; in fact, I'm one of the lucky ones. I found a way to make a career that was flexible and remote, one I could scale up or down as I needed to. However, plenty of military spouses don't have that same luck, and many struggle to figure out to what extent their career fits into their lives and their spouse's career trajectory.

Since starting my own career journey working remotely, I've owned my own business for 11 years, but I've also worked in high-level and high-paying roles as a remote marketing director and now as a Chief Operations Officer at Advanced Amazon Ads. What I share in this chapter is built not just on my own experience of growing a remote career, but what I've picked up from mentoring many military spouses along the way.

So many military spouses want to have a career but face an uphill battle in figuring out how to do that. There are systemic barriers and unique challenges that hold them back from being able to work the way they want to.

Challenges Facing Military Spouses Moving Frequently

One of the most substantial barriers that military spouses face is simply that they move so often. While employers shouldn't discriminate against military spouses in the hiring process, some do if they have an awareness of the military moving frequency or have hired military spouses in the past. They may be hesitant to bring on someone for an in-person role when that individual may move in a year or just a few years later. This means that military spouses who are otherwise qualified and would make great employees often get overlooked in the application process.

Although the COVID-19 pandemic and the resulting surge in remote work opportunities have made this somewhat less of an issue, many spouses are still employed in hybrid or in-person roles, where this could be a concern when submitting an application. Although an employer will not likely come out directly and tell you that you were not hired because you are a military spouse, these conversations may happen behind closed doors. Some military spouses choose not to bring up their partner's active duty status and hide things such as photos on social media that would otherwise give this information away.

Although it is unfortunate that some employers may discriminate in this manner, military spouses attempting to take control of their career and to improve their chances of receiving a position may wish to take these steps if they believe it would be helpful to keep the conversation focused on their skills and abilities in the potential role rather than their partner's active duty career.

Military spouses move frequently due to their partner's careers. In addition, many military spouses have to alter their schedules and be adjustable and flexible when partners undertake training or other opportunities that represent short-term disruptions. Job opportunities are not equal at every single base, meaning that plenty of military spouses may have to take a step back and work in positions where they are underemployed. Many other spouses are unable to find employment at all, especially if they work in a specialized career field or are at a higher level position, such as an executive role.

Along with moving so many times, it can be hard to finish or take up an education program when you need to fit that into an existing schedule or aren't sure whether or not you'll live in an area long enough to wrap up a program.

When married to someone in the service, that service always takes priority and can make it difficult for a spouse to find a career that adapts and grows with them. The military is in control of where you live, what your partner does, their schedule, their pay, and so much more. While there are certainly plenty of benefits to becoming part of a military marriage or a military family, the challenges often catch spouses of all ages, educational backgrounds, and career types off guard.

The network of other military spouses can be a very valuable place to turn to when looking for ways to navigate your own career field. Speaking to others who have been through this path before can help illuminate you regarding the options and help you decide on as much of a flexible arrangement as you may need.

Bear in mind that over the course of your partner's time in the military, you may alter your career goals and want something different. For example, it is common for some spouses to do something known as geobatching, which involves the non-military partner and potentially any children to stay in one duty station or another geographic location while the active service member goes on their next permanent change of station move for a year or longer.

Licensing and certification concerns

Some military spouses work in fields that require specific statewide or regional licenses. Examples include attorneys and teachers, although there are many more. While some states do have reciprocity programs or streamlined application programs that allow military spouses to more easily obtain their new licensure and ability to carry forward their career in a new state, this is not always the case.

It can add an additional layer of stress for a military spouse who is preparing for a PCS when they must also worry about submitting appropriate application materials in time.

There are resource networks out there to help military spouses with certain aspects of licensing, such as in the teaching or legal community. However, since so many can vary from one state to another, it's important to look for these networks as far in advance of your move as you can.

Taking time off of work

For a range of reasons that run the spectrum from everything including intentionally taking time out of the workplace to raise a family, to care for elderly loved ones, to deal with a health crisis, or to support your spouse's military career, all the way up to people who need flexibility in their role due to shifting training schedules and childcare responsibilities in the present, there are many different reasons why military spouses may have gaps on their resume.

Many military spouses struggle with a crisis of confidence when it comes to seeking a job and putting themself forward through the application process. These gaps in resumes and work periods can only make things more difficult, as the spouse feels as though they're required to explain why they took time off or have gaps of months or even years within their resume between positions.

One of the easiest ways to tackle this problem is to focus more on what you have done in the here and now. Working through internships, mentorships, online certifications, additional education, and volunteer opportunities help refocus the conversation on your resume and with any potential employer about the efforts you're taking now. Being upfront and honest about taking time out of the workplace and keeping this to a simple sentence or two should it come up in a conversation or in a cover letter is beneficial.

At the end of the day, most employers want employees who will do a great job in their position at work, and these employers are less concerned about life circumstances that may have led you to think differently about your career in the past. Do not feel ashamed of any decisions you have made that were right for you, your family, or your marriage, and do not feel as though you need to justify these in great detail to anyone either.

Know that gaps on your resume is especially common throughout the military community, but that these are certainly not the only employees active on the job market who are coping with this challenge. Showing how you have put in effort now and continue to put in effort throughout your job search brings the conversation forward to a more positive focus.

Addressing Spouse Challenges in Remote Work: What You Can Do How to leverage remote work opportunities

Some spouses wish to continue working in person even if their partner moves to a new duty station. But others could benefit from the potential greater stability offered by remote work opportunities. Remote work opportunities may already exist at a company that has a remote first or a hybrid culture but can also be brought up to an employer who has not yet considered the benefits of keeping part of their team or even a single member of their team remote.

If you wish to take your in-person position remotely, do not ask your employer if they are willing to do this without first coming to the table with a proposal of your own. You would need to be able to illustrate how solid of an employee you've been up to this point already and how you would overcome any potential challenges moving somewhere else and working as a remote member of the team, such as staying engaged in the work culture, dealing with time zone differences, asynchronous communication and more.

If you are able to come to your employer with a compelling proposition that shows how you could continue contributing to the team and assist them with keeping stability by maintaining you on the existing team, they are much more likely to agree to work with you.

Note that you do not have to work for someone else in order to work remotely. You can also start your own business. However, this path is filled with its own pros and cons. I started my remote career this way and then leveraged that experienced into executive remote job roles.

How to support other military spouses in their careers

Anyone who is gainfully employed either working for themselves or for another company may have specific insights that can be very beneficial to other military spouses. There are a variety of ways that we can all help one another within this community to help ensure that military spouses continue to have access to employment opportunities.

The more we can help one another, the better. We can all contribute in ways that help alleviate the challenges military spouses face when trying to break into remote work.

Here is a rundown of the various ways that you can support other military spouses.

Have a conversation with your local representatives about military spouse employment issues.

Despite the fact that military spouse employment has been an issue for some time, plenty of elected officials and legislators are unfamiliar with the problem. Letting them know about your position as a military spouse makes you a valued member of their constituency but also calls their attention to ways that they may be able to help this specific community.

The more advocates we have speaking up about military spouse and military family issues, the higher the likelihood that there is greater awareness around these concerns and that we can begin to have meaningful conversations, program development at the corporation level, educational support, continuations, and more.

Share your story

This is one way I'm giving back directly through this book. I know that for me seeing other people be able to build their own remote work careers showed me that it was possible. It inspired me to reach out to them to talk to them and apply these learnings to my own path. You have no idea how inspirational your own story may be for someone else, whether it's sharing in a Facebook group how you tackled a tough interview question or the steps you took to land a new gig before you PCSed with your spouse. Sometimes, all we need is to know that someone else is lending a helping hand!

Volunteer with organizations that support mil spouse efforts

You can also get more involved at the local, regional, or national level by partnering with organizations that help military spouses start their own businesses or land career positions. You contribute as an advocate in this way, but may also be able to support full-scale programs or individual spouses.

Starting internship, mentoring, or job shadow opportunities

You may also be able to provide one-to-one support to military spouses in your community by setting up this program individually or working with your employer to create one.

In many cases, spouses just need a foot in the door, and by working to create an internship, job shadow, or mentorship program that allows them to get some experience and determine if a career with your company or a career in your field is right for them and does a great deal of good for the community overall.

It could just be the first step a military spouse needs to start their own or grow a career. Think about how you may be able to give back.

Help Spouses 1:1

Providing one-to-one support for resume development, interview practice, or job application assistance. Applying for jobs, whether they are in person or remote, can be a taxing situation. I had to apply to well over 90 positions before receiving my first full-time remote job offer, and it was disheartening to make it all the way through the interview process to watch someone else be selected or to learn after I submitted to a job I was really excited about that the pay was not in line with what I needed.

Simply providing moral support is helpful, but you can often go a lot further by giving job interview assistance and other one-on-one help for military spouses actively seeking employment.

This can also include providing insight and guidance related to things like preparing for certification exams or tailoring a resume for applicant tracking systems.

As military spouses, we can all work together to help improve issues surrounding military employment, whether it's providing resources to someone, one-on-one support, recommending a program at your company, or advocating with legislators. Many military spouses have busy schedules, and I know that I felt that being on the other side of this with my own employment and insight into the entire process of finding and getting remote jobs made me feel a responsibility to give back to the community.

You do not need to give back to the community in a big way to have an impact, but it can be especially beneficial to reach out your hand to offer to help others who are looking to take the first steps with their career or regain some of the traction they had in a prior position.

As military spouses, veterans, and other members of the military community, we can all help lift up one another.

Chapter Two

Be A Hawk- Betsy Moore Nelson

This chapter is dedicated in remembrance of 1 Lt Luke "Stiff" Johnson and in honor of our amazing 23d Fighter Squadron Family. Always there. I also want to dedicate this to and thank my dear, dear friend, Cathy Theisen - who helped keep me sane when the world seemed to be crumbling around me. I did not want to move to Columbus AFB, but I would not have met Cathy. Friends Forever!

My name is Betsy Nelson, and as an Air Force wife, I'd like to share some insights. While some of the stories I'll share may seem daunting and could potentially discourage you from pursuing a relationship with someone in the military, that is not my intention. Deaths, accidents, and miscommunication are challenges that exist both in civilian and military life. However, the implications of mistakes in a military setting can be more severe.

Despite these challenges, our military is the best trained and most professional in the world. I would gladly go through it all again. When you weigh the pros and cons, the pros overwhelmingly prevail. I feel honored to be part of someone's life who has willingly chosen to prioritize his life, family, and livelihood for his country—an uncommon commitment that many civilian families may not fully comprehend.

Having been raised in a military family, with my father serving as a career Naval officer, I thought I understood military life. However, the modern Air Force differs significantly from the Navy of the 50s, 60s, and 70s. While my childhood memories are filled with calls, Christmas cards, and visits from my parents' friends worldwide, the romanticized portrayal of military life in movies does not entirely align with reality.

Despite the challenges, all military members are heroes who have willingly committed themselves to serve. They put their country before life and family, and we, as spouses, are left to navigate the consequences and frustrations that come with it.

For some, their loved ones have paid the ultimate price. Regardless of the outcome, all spouses have raised their hands, expressing a willingness to give their lives for an ideal—an act uniquely American and one that fills me with pride. The consequences include long days and nights, deployments, and unplanned TDYs. Frustrations arise from often living in old, cramped quarters on base, not necessarily in the best part of town, and not having control over where we live due to the dictates of the Air Force.

The military family doesn't always get it right, just as our blood family sometimes falls short. I've experienced a range of support, from less than desirable to the most fantastic. Rather than dwelling on the negative, I want to focus on the positive. Understanding how your role in the military family can make a significant difference in someone's life is crucial.

By sharing our amazing experiences, I hope to highlight the joy they bring. As a spouse, recognizing the impact you can have on someone's time on station is essential. Reach out to others as a friend and a member of the broader military family, as your actions can truly make a difference.

In Merriam-Webster's lexicon, the term "family" encompasses the notion of a "clan" — a collective with shared ancestry — and "fellowship" — a group united by common convictions or affiliations. Life presents us with multiple familial circles: our blood relations, church community, work colleagues, and notably, our military family.

Among these, the military family forges some of the most enduring bonds. Living on bases, our children attend the same schools, our spouses work side by side, and we navigate the highs and lows of life collectively, whether in celebration or mourning. The demanding nature of military life, operating 24/7, blurs the lines between work and personal life, posing a unique challenge to achieving a harmonious "work-life balance."

While striving for this equilibrium, living off-base can inadvertently distance us from the military family network. In contrast to the broader American population, where individuals often reside within a modest distance from their mothers, military spouses stand as outliers. With over 2 million uniformed military members and 2.6 million family members, this community represents less than 1.5% of the nation. The rarity and distinctiveness of military life become apparent when contrasting with World War II, where 16 million Americans served, constituting around 20% of the population and touching nearly every family. The military family holds a unique and crucial role in today's landscape.

Across various assignments, only one squadron managed to achieve a perfect balance. Others varied in their success, some falling short, while others were commendable but not flawless. The pursuit of contentment as a military spouse hinges significantly on personal effort, yet the company we keep can profoundly influence our perception of each assignment. In real estate, the mantra is "Location, Location, Location," but in the military, it is undeniably about the people.

The quality of relationships and connections cultivated during deployments and day-to-day life can make or break the overall experience for a military spouse. Thus, in the intricate tapestry of military life, the importance of the military family cannot be overstated.

While Paul and I were on our way to Fort Worth in 2023 for the 23rd Fighter Squadron 2023 Reunion, I was asked to be part of this collaboration. That was no accident. After a weekend of recounting stories - both happy and sad; so, sharing how the fighter squadron family reduces the risk of "no one left behind" is perfect for this chapter.

A standard part of a flying squadron is the squadron bar (now known as a Heritage Room). I did not know anything about the "squadron bar" until we moved to Spangdahlem AB, Germany, and my husband became the SME (Squadron Medical Element) for the 23rd Fighter Squadron. Once I understood the importance of the squadron bar, my understanding of taking care of families - no spouse or family left behind - became solidified in how I felt we should do things.

Fighter squadrons are a rare bird—no pun intended. The pilot's job is stressful and dangerous. Within a year, we lost three friends in training accidents. Not that accidents don't happen in other career fields, but flying—especially single-seat aircraft—is inherently dangerous. For this reason, the flying squadron literally becomes a family.

I must start by telling you that I was not happy the first time Paul said he was going to the squadron bar instead of coming home after work. He couldn't even tell me how long he would be. An extra 30 minutes for one beer? Or many beers over many hours? Should Lacy and I eat or wait? There was an argument and lots of tears. I lost the argument - but that was a good thing. That night was the beginning of what is now decades of trust between the pilots and my husband. They are all retired now, but they call my husband for advice and help with their son's and daughter's medical issues in the Air Force.

When we arrived at Spangdahlem AB, Germany (the 52nd Fighter Wing) in the summer of 1999, there were three fighter squadrons: the 22d and 23d (F16s) and the 81st (A10s). Not long after the night of our argument, Paul flew for the first time in the backseat of one of the four F16-D models - known as the "family model" because it has a backseat for training (or the flight doc). That day was not memorable because of the fun experience of seeing Paul land and the excitement of his first F-16 flight; it was memorable because the A-10 landing just before he was supposed to…crashed on the runway. (The pilot ejected and was okay.)

The events surrounding all this were not smooth from the standpoint of the way things should have happened - primarily the notice to families that there was a mishap and your loved one is okay. First, I received a call from someone looking for Paul, who knew about the crash but did not have any details except "there's been a crash." Seriously. I was about to leave the house with our 5-year-old daughter to attend choir practice.

Next, my route to practice took me by the section of the runway where the crashed A-10 was. At that point, I didn't know it was an A-10 (there are not any A-10s with a backseat). When I got to choir practice, I was visibly shaken, and one of the other ladies' husbands was a pilot, so she called to find out what had happened. Had there been a problem that had been bad news, I was with my friends from the Chapel, including one of the chaplain's wives. The pilot's wife reported back that an A-10 crashed, the pilot was okay, and all the other F-16s that were about to land were diverted to a German fighter base in northern Germany. Everyone was okay.

Paul eventually got home around midnight; he was supposed to have landed around 2:30 pm. It was a long day, and I was very upset, to say the least. I was not angry with him, but he got the point and let the squadron commander know how upset I was.

What should have happened: all the wives (at the time, all the pilots were males) whose husbands were flying that day that there was a problem/mishap, and their husbands were fine but got a call saying they would be late getting home. In civilian terms, Paul was not manifested on the plane that day, so I did not get a call. Spoiler alert: that never happened again. Fortunately, it never happened because there was not a reason for a call to be made - at least not when Paul was flying.

To this day, his commander at the time apologizes to me when he sees me. He knew the importance of communication and family. He knew how he'd feel if his wife had not gotten a call. Regardless of the comings and goings of commanders, pilots, and families at the 23rd FS, we looked after each other. And we still do to this day. Always will; family.

Yes, living in western Germany in an idyllic small town at a single-mission fighter base didn't hurt. But again, it's the people. Sadly, most of our assignments did not involve the tight-knit family we experienced at Spangdahlem AB. But because it was fairly early in our military career, we learned from the best how to be supportive to our Air Force and military family for the next 18 years.

Those pesky quotes

"The Air Force phrase, 'If the Air Force wanted you to have a family, it would have issued you one,' humorously captures the unique challenges faced by military families. It is often said that the hardest job in the military is being a military spouse. While this statement holds some truth, it's not as simple as a yes or no.

Service members with fulfilling family lives tend to perform exceptionally well in their duties. Conversely, challenges at home can translate into problems at work. Recognizing this, the military has a vested interest in ensuring the well-being and happiness of its families.

Also, I doubt it was harder for me than my husband when he was in Afghanistan, but I won't argue that it was harder for me when he was home - because most of the time when his body was home, his mind and sentiment were not. He had a lot to balance - husband, father, commander, doctor, officer, mentor, etc. Again - the large number of responsibilities are not exclusive to the military - but they manifest themselves in a daily manner that can cause added stress on a marriage and a family.

The definition of a family and roles in the family have changed a lot in the decade between my father's retirement and my husband's commissioning; thus, I knew being a military spouse would be different for me than it was for my mother. My father had 10 assignments in 20 years - and his last assignment was five and a half years; that's nine assignments in fourteen and a half years. That's a lot of moving - especially in an era when transportation was more difficult and took longer than it does now. Flying is easier and quicker now, and communication is definitely easier.

During some deployed locations, it's possible to FaceTime, Zoom, and use other apps for instant communication, a far cry from the letters my parents wrote to each other to and from a ship on the other side of the world. Now, when many military spouses work, balancing the stress of being a deployed parent and being a single mom or dad while working can be daunting. Another reason we need to make sure we fulfill our part as the best military friend/family member we can.

We, as spouses, are not martyrs, but we do sacrifice. A LOT! It makes me proud. I can't speak for my kids, but military kids sacrifice a lot, too. They go to new schools every few years and have to pick up, leave friends, and adapt to new environments at a moment's notice. We, as spouses, do, too, with our friends and, for some, co-workers. We stay back and "guard the homefront."

When people thank me for my service, I'm embarrassed but honored. As parents, we deal with the consequences of uprooting our children - often alone. Being a single parent in reality or because your spouse is not "there" is very stressful, but it can also bring you closer to your children. Children are resilient and can thrive in a world without stability (many military brats follow in their parent's footsteps!) - but they take their lead from their parents. If we have a positive attitude, they likely will as well.

So, what does it mean to be "left behind?"

Being left behind can be abandonment. It can be a handicap. It can mean to be forgotten. Reflecting on President George W. Bush's "No Child Left Behind (NCLB)" policy reveals its shortcomings. While the intention was to ensure equal opportunities and quality education for all children, the focus on metrics overshadowed the importance of allocating resources for achieving these goals.

Similarly, as a military spouse, I find parallels in the inadequacies of existing programs aimed at supporting families like mine. Resume-building classes and help with job hunting are great, but building a support network - a family - is what really counts. Using the Family Support Center programs is a great jumping off point - show up and participate. But don't stop there. Make friends and continue to be engaged with your military family outside of formal programs. This will definitely lessen the chance that you get "left behind."

Don't forget lipstick before going to the Commissary.

As the daughter of Southerners and a Naval Officer from the 50s, 60s, and 70s, I was taught from a very early age to look "right" when I left the house. My mom stopped me a few decades ago when we were home for a visit as I was heading to Walmart to grab a few things - "You can't leave the house looking like that!" She meant - I was in jeans, a t-shirt, and hair in a pony-tail, and probably no make-up. I might run into someone she knows. It's not necessarily any different in the military - especially when my husband was a commander - Even a quick trip to the Commissary demanded a polished appearance. Sadly, appearances can matter - even though they shouldn't.

As military spouses, the pressure to always be "on" can be overwhelming. I fell into that trap. Paul was commissioned in May 1989, and we married in August 1990. It wasn't until the fall of 2010 that I was finally able to free myself from feeling judged when doing things for my family. It's not that I quit caring how I looked. While I still care about my public appearance, I no longer let societal expectations dictate my choices, even on hectic days.

We are all more comfortable being ourselves; and we are more successful in life when being ourselves. I truly care how I look in public - but sometimes we are in a hurry or life handed us just too many challenges on that day. And that's okay. I spent 20 years being "Paul's wife," "Doc's wife," "VooDoo's wife," "the Boss's wife," etcetera, on top of "Lacy's Mom" and "Matthew's mom." By the way, I loved being all of those! But first - I'm Betsy. I can't be successful at fulfilling those other roles unless I'm true to myself. And back to family - they love you for who you are, not a title. It took me two decades to realize that being true to oneself is key to personal success.

Some of my truisms

1. Have a personal slogan. Mine is "Leave a place better than you found it." That steered me to people and activities wherever we lived that aligned with my personal, moral beliefs. Families look after each other.

2. Be kind to everyone. A pilot cannot just get in a jet and have it fly. It needs fuel, it needs maintenance, it needs a navigator or a working navigation system. The Air Force and military need everyone - enlisted, officer, civilians, contractors, and FAMILIES! We all make the big machine work. When one cog is broken, the machine is inefficient at best, and broken, at worst. Families work best together.

3. Enjoy your community. Yeah - some places are harder than others. I remember in the ROTC lounge at Ole Miss hearing the "Best and Worst Bases" list. "Why not Minot? Freezing the Reason." We have known quite a lot of people who loved Minot. Realistically because of the weather. They depend on each other and build strong relationships. Families take care of each other.

4. Be involved in your local community. If you live on base, which we did for over 17 ½ years, leave the base. Get involved in the kids' schools. Join a civic club. Do volunteer work. I promise it will make or break your time at that duty station. When you meet locals, you build relationships and learn that it's not about places, but about people. Families help each other.

5. I'm going to take a hit for this one, but - join the Spouses' Club. Seriously. I know it seems old-fashioned or an "elitist" club for the Chiefs 'wives and retired Generals 'wives. I'm not going to lie, there is some of that. But the Spouses Clubs do a lot of good on the base - and we all benefit from it. They raise A LOT of money for college scholarships for graduating seniors and spouses. They run the Thrift Shop - a huge deal for younger families, especially in harder economic times. Also - BINGO! There are fun mini-clubs, and you will find lots of new friends. The modern Spouses Clubs usually rotate between lunch and evening meetings, so working spouses can attend every other month - or stay-at-home spouses can go in the evening once the member comes home to stay with the kids. Families spend time together.

6. Invite your neighbors over for dinner or plan a block party. We live in a world where people are busy, and sadly, we don't always get to know our neighbors. A potluck on a Saturday or Sunday afternoon is loved by all, and kids will rule the party! Don't go through military life alone. Families fellowship together.

If you're reading this because you're dating or engaged to a military member or someone contemplating military life - DO NOT be dismayed. There are ups and downs in life - regardless of your age, job, or station in life. Military life throws us lots of lemons. Sometimes, the lemonade is perfect, sometimes it's a little too bitter.

I opened this chapter with the definition of family. Here's another definition for you...Merriam-Webster defines a bureaucracy as a body of nonelected government officials. b. : an administrative policymaking group. 2. : government characterized by specialization of functions, adherence to fixed rules, and a hierarchy of authority.

You, as a military spouse, have to function within a chaotic bureaucracy - but Merriam-Webster's definition may not capture the challenges you face. The bureaucracy of the military is likely what makes everyone so cranky and their jobs "so difficult." The military bureaucracy is not a beautiful thing - except in war - it actually functions exceptionally well when literally "at war." When at home - things are less defined. Understanding the bureaucracy is different from the people is important - and having that understanding friend (military family!) to vent to over coffee or an adult beverage will help you get to the next day.

My friend, Cathy, as I mentioned in my dedication, is responsible for many, many of those days when I needed to vent so I could make it to the next day. Cathy and I met in the summer of 2006 at Columbus AFB, Mississippi. Columbus is decidedly NOT a garden spot, but I wouldn't trade anything to have missed that assignment. That assignment put Cathy in my life, and not many days go by that we don't text or call. Both of our husbands are retired. All our kids are grown. But we still need each other. Everyone needs a Cathy in their life; seek out yours. She will enrich your life and allow you to enrich hers as well.

Dual-Agency in the Military Family

Understanding our spouses can make or break our relationship. If our spouse has a career field that is not sensitive and he can talk openly about his work/frustrations/co-workers, things are definitely easier - like those who work in "benign" civilian careers. Many of our spouses, though, have careers that are sensitive. Some may work in fields requiring a security clearance; some may work in medicine, law, or chaplaincy.

My husband was an Air Force physician. Not until about five years before his retirement did he fully begin to be aware of the "dual agency" he lived in. With the help of a senior Chaplain, they began to write about how to successfully be both at the same time - Physician/Officer, Chaplain/Officer, JAG/Officer. Are you a doctor first ("first do no harm") or are you an officer first ("take down the enemy").

When Paul deployed in 2010 to the Helmand Province, I walked with him to the jet at Fairchild AFB. He was carrying a small black box with a handle, and I asked what it was. "My sidearm." I was aghast that a doctor would carry a gun. He was there to save lives, not take them. His response was that his duty was to protect his patients. That I get, but it also opened a window for me to see the inner conflict a dual-agency professional deals with. Would a chaplain shoot someone to protect himself or another soldier?

Dual-agency is complicated, and these issues are present in relationships outside of work. Most military members cannot "turn off" the military. They don't serve 9-5, Monday through Friday. It's 24/7/365 for everyone. That means they are never really turned off of work at home, and neither is their spouse.

We were, honestly, oblivious to this for most of Paul's career. Even as a retiree, he continues to write about dual-agency; what oath takes precedence? I still see his inner struggle. We talk about it - which I'm grateful for. We started and finished as a team, and now we want to make sure we can help other families do the same, especially those who deal with some of the same professional issues we did. If your spouse is a dual-agency professional, keep the lines of communication open. Gently find out what role he's playing; knowing that will help communication at home!

Dealing with a spouse with Moral Injury

What is Moral Injury? Moral injury isn't talked about much. It's an unseen wound like PTSD. Paul came home from his last deployment to Afghanistan with moral injury. But like dual-agency, he wasn't really aware of it for a while. I cannot fathom what he or our brave Soldiers, Sailors, Airmen, and Marines have seen. Learning to help them heal from a moral injury ("I lived, but my buddy died.") takes as much work as helping them heal from a physical wound - probably more.

My husband is still dealing with how to overcome his moral injury even years after retirement; hence, I'm dealing with it as well. Like mental health issues, moral injury affects the entire family. The military family - especially the service members 'coworkers - those he was deployed with - are vital to his recovery. His blood family means well and wants him to free himself of it - but they can't help. Even I can only do so much - be supportive, listen, and validate that it's okay to have those feelings. But his fellow Airmen, Soldiers, Sailors, and Marines understand. They are the family that supports through shared understanding. They have been there. They are the military family I have been talking about.

It's wonderful to have our real family near or accessible. But many times, for military families, it's our military family that really does the most for us. Your in-laws love your spouse and would do anything for him/her. But they cannot empathize with him regarding PTSD, moral injury, or what he saw or did on deployment (or for that matter a training accident). But our spouse's shipmates, squadronmates, platoon mates, etcetera can; and do. We must give them the space to do just that. Once again, we rely on our military family. We can. And we should.

Be A Hawk!

I titled this chapter "Be A Hawk." The 23rd Fighter Squadron mascot is the hawk. The 23rd means a lot to me. Being a Hawk means to be part of an amazing family. It means to circle over others and watch over them, protect them. According to www.theraptortrust.org, hawks are strong and powerful. Also, "Their sense of hearing is excellent, and their eyesight the best in the entire animal world. Not only can hawks see greater distances than humans, but their visual acuity (the ability to see clearly) is eight times that of ours."

Clearly, the 23rd FS was aptly named. They certainly encompassed taking care of family through heightened senses and seeing clearly. Being able to see through the bureaucracy and static in life to know when a family member is in need is a special talent.

Conclusion

About that bar...earlier, I mentioned Paul's first visit to the squadron bar. That evening was one of the most important nights in his career. He began to integrate into the squadron family, building trust as a co-worker and friend - not just the guy who could "ground" pilots at a whim. That relationship-building literally allowed him to save lives and careers. And because the squadron trusted him and brought him into the squadron family - I was brought in as well. And that is very profound!

Our 23rd Fighter Squadron Family became our closest friends. We survived a squadron baby boom in 2000 and leaned on each other as we mourned the loss of a pilot in 2002. As importantly, we were always there for the in-between times: carpools, sick children, ski trips, babysitting, and all the things that pop up in life we need "to phone a friend."

If that "family feel" doesn't exist in your squadron, you can help create it. Set up a potluck. Suggest a family day at the zoo. Plan a ski trip or camping trip. Balance family time with your military family, and don't forget to have adult time with your military family. Sometimes, we need to have grown-up conversations. Our kids grew up with lots of friends they knew they could depend on because their parents depended on each other.

Sometimes I remembered the sugar, sometimes a friend or co-worker of my husband remembered the sugar, and sometimes the lemonade was just straight bitter. But life was sweetest with our military family there to support us and us to support them. Be there with some sugar and be a Hawk!

Chapter Three

A Spouse Is A Spouse- Sara Copp

I will never forget my first experience with "those" military spouses at the Spouse's Club lunch; it's etched in my mind like a scene from a movie. You see- and bare with me here, my service member and I were dual military- yes, I was a soldier. Did I lose you? If you're still with me here- awesome.

Okay… at the risk of sounding "stuck up," or whatever people think when they hear this and losing the other half of you- I was an officer, and a Company Commander, but before you go paging to the next chapter thinking, now we definitely have nothing in common- I want to challenge you to stay… and in case it's any consolation prize to anyone who has just written me off- I joined the Army as at 17, as a shiny PVT, a big fat e-nothing, so believe me, I 100% understand what it feels like to be on both sides enlisted, and a spouse! Okay– back to the story…

We had just PCS'd, my husband was already knee-deep into work and had zero time for me, and left me to unpack the house alone. I had zero friends (sound familiar?!- see, I told you we'd get along) We were in Leavenworth, Kansas– Not exactly a budding Metropolitan (no offense to anyone who is heading there.

It's a great small base & perfect if you have a family, but it's really lame if you're kid-free and don't have the luxury of driving to Kanas City every weekend because of your husband's work). I desperately wanted friends- and unfortunately, since I was in charge of everyone who worked with me, or they were in charge of me, work "friends" were out, too. So, I signed up for my first Military Spouse event, a Spouse's Club Luncheon. (cue the eye roll)

I had just pulled Superman/Clark Kent quick change in the bathroom of the lunch place; I packed a tee-length cotton dress, some dressy sandals, and a Coach purse (I mean, I think that's what officers' wives wear to Spouses' Luncheons right?!). I quickly looked around to see if anyone was in there, and when the coast was clear, I went into the stall, removed my uniform, threw on the dress, and tried as hard as I could to rub those terrible green sock lines imprints away from my ankles.

I took a deep breath, walked out & looked in the mirror at my hair in my side part, and my slicked to my head hair pulled into a tight sock bun. I did my best to tussle the sides of my hair to give a little movement to that hairstyle because it is a dead giveaway, threw on some lip gloss, and that was it. I shoved my Army uniform and clunky boots under the sink and walked out to the registration table.

I know you're probably thinking- why didn't you just wear your uniform- no one would have cared. I'm sure you're probably right- but 2013 Sara really wasn't convinced, and the following events really echoed that insecurity.

I grabbed my name tag and walked into the snake pit... I mean the mingling area. The base commander's wife, and his second-in-command's wife. I didn't know who anyone was- and frankly, I didn't care, but there was A LOT of ass kissing going on (puke).

There was an insanely long line of older women standing next to fancier older women, shaking our hands. We had to say our names and where our spouses worked(double puke). I guess I was thankful they were like, "And what's your husband's rank? It felt very formal and unnecessary. A dog and pony show- if this was 10 years earlier, I bet they'd all be wearing white gloves.

Fort Leavenworth has a 10-month Mid Level Officer School, Leadership & masters program, as well as Center for Combine Arms & Army Doctrine. Aka, the people who write all the "official how the Army does everything books & the Standard Operation Procedure (SOPs)... (The mecca of what "right looks like").

It's also a HUB for International Exchange Officers, as well as various inter-branch officers(Navy, Marines, Coast Guard, and even FBI. Other 3 Letter Agencies can go to that school, oh, and probably what it's most famous for it's two large correctional facilities. Lots of High Brass- and very few enlisted on Fort Leavenworth. I think there is something insane like four 3 Star Generals living on that tiny post.

Most of these spouses were here for CGSC (The Command and General Staff College, the same school my husband was here for, so I felt like I was in the same boat as most of these ladies. A few people complimented me on my purse and asked me where we came from and what branch my husband was in; the basic pleasantries.

I found myself in a circle of ladies. All of us had drinks in our hands, and we were talking about our movers, our damage, and the progress we've made unpacking. Some of us were talking about our pets and their previous duty stations, and most of us were chatting about how annoyed we were with the commentary about how this was going to be the " best year of our lives," yet we were already seeing less and less of our spouses.

Someone got on the topic of working. 2013 Sara didn't know this was a sore subject for military spouses. Most of them sold some sort of MLM or had a photography business or something, and one of them asked me, what do you do, Sara, I said, "Oh, I work at the hospital," I replied casually, but the reaction on her face wasn't what I expected. "How did you manage to land a job there?" she quizzed, and suddenly, I realized the chasm between us. Crap! School just started. We just got here- how was I going to explain this… I was exposed, and I fumbled, "Oh, my job just transferred."

"Oh, that's really strange," she said. I put in my transfer four months ago, and I haven't heard anything; who did you go through?" She named the lady in our HR—I must have turned white. I am a really bad liar. I tried to play cool and remain vague.

I said, "oh, well, my old boss at the hospital I was working at Fort Campbell, talked to my incoming boss because my husband was coming here, and they got me a position." (Which was 100% true, that is exactly what happened) but I didn't realize that wasn't how things happened in the civilian world because civilian Jobs had to go through USA Jobs- and like literally you need a magic wand, and a medium & lucky leprechaun for your resume to make it past USA Jobs electronic gatekeeper. She went on to say- in a heat of anger and frustration that she couldn't believe that I got a job and she hadn't heard anything.

I said sheepishly, "oh well, I'm in the Army, they usually try and make it work for us. As soon as the words "in the Army" left my lips- it was like the record player screeched and the music stopped, every one of them gave me a disgusted look; like I was the enemy.

It was like I wanted their husbands, or I wasn't just sitting around having a good conversation about the frustrations of the workload our husbands were already doing, and I'd set off an invisible stink bomb. They subtly turned away and scattered, heading to different corners of the room. I was so mortified. Maybe it wasn't as dramatic as I remember, but that's how it felt at that moment.

I don't remember the rest of the event, but I do remember that I tried again the next month. I was determined to make friends- honestly, I just needed someone to talk to - and I was so incredibly lonely. We had been at Fort Campbell for 4 years, and I had met so many close girlfriends. We were all living a dual-military life- and I truly missed having a group of girls to connect with. Side note: we were definitely not the GI Jane type of soldiers; all of us were pretty girly outside of our uniforms. I didn't really deem them any different than the group of girls

I hung out with in college or those I hung out with in high school. I was so hopeful that one of these spouses' events would connect me with some friends.

It became a pattern to avoid mentioning my job at the next set of spouse events. I would not make that mistake again. If pushed, I'd toss in a vague mention of working in hospital administration. For months, I'd break from work, dash to the golf club's restroom, stow away my uniform and boots, and slip into a sundress. It felt like leading a double life. Until one day, one of them sent me a text.

"You don't just work at the hospital… YOUR PICTURE IS ON THE COMMAND WALL OF THE HOSPITAL!!! It's a good picture, too!! OMG. I can't believe it! I know you- you're like famous- and I had no idea."

Busted. Well, at least that friend still loves me to this day!

Looking back, I chuckle at my eagerness to blend in. Why did I strive so hard to fit in? If only I could have told that younger version of myself that she didn't need to pretend. I wasn't confident with myself. Making friends as an adult is REALLY hard. All the mean girl high school b.s. comes back with a vengeance.

My spouse's time at Leavenworth ended with a surprise—my husband would be deploying, and I would be staying for another six months to finish out my second year in command. Oh…and I found out I was pregnant.

Nothing prepares you for a deployment- and even though this was our third one (fourth if you're counting mine) together, it doesn't ever get easier. Add being pregnant- 1,000s miles away from friends and family, and all your friends have just PCS'd. The last thing I wanted to do was make new friends. So I didn't; instead- I became a hermit.

Maybe it was nesting, or maybe I just needed an artist outlet- but I started obsessively thrift shopping, and I taught myself how to machine embroider. I turned into a craft supply hoarder, which was neither healthy for my bank account nor my sanity, but it was fun.

Being pregnant was hard on me mentally. I was so bitter that I had to do it alone and I was so bitter he was missing all the movements. He wasn't there to get me ice cream or rub my feet. I was bitter that I didn't get to choose my doctor or that I never got to see the same doctor twice. I was especially bitter when I was told that I had to go TDY to Texas for three months while pregnant on my own in the middle of my command for training.

Everyone told me I couldn't run or drink coffee- (DUDE… don't tell a 1st time-pregnant athlete coffee drinker this). This was what broke that camel's back & spun me into a deep depression and helped me to gain 75 pounds– that never came off.

Oh yeah, and have PCS- Solo, all while being pregnant, and then do all unpacking and getting ready for the baby– all by yourself. Yeah. 0 stars, do not recommended. If you do ever find yourself in this predicament or worse- I 100% know you can do it. It will 100% suck, but just know- I will be rooting for you- and I know you will be able to do it. It is 1,000% okay to cry and eat whatever you want or not unpack and just buy new if you want because you're pregnant by yourself and doing it all, and you are freaking amazing.

Having a baby- in a military community was literally the best thing that ever happened to me. My husband was TDY for deployments overseas a lot & made it home just a few days before I gave birth- and was gone again when she was three months old (see all these similarities we have).

After I had my daughter, I joined a Military Spouse Mommy and Me Fitness Group while I was on maternity leave called iStroll, where moms bring their kids and work out with them. At six weeks, I showed up with my marketplace jogging stroller and started class. I probably shouldn't have been working out, but I was so ready to, and I didn't recognize myself anymore.

This was exact the group I had been looking for. Everyone was so nice, we went out for coffee after class, and the kids all played with each other- since my daughter just napped during class- I got to talk to other moms; it was the best thing ever… and then I had to go back to work. I would attend class on the weekends, but after a few months- almost no one recognized me, and I started to feel like an outsider again. So I did what I did in Leavenworth and became a recluse- which was a terrible idea, but I didn't know what else to do.

At eight weeks, my daughter got pink eye at daycare- and I spent most of my lunch breaks with her on the floor of her daycare. I pumped twice a day at work in a storage closet with two folding chairs and an outlet, and I barely saw my daughter awake except at 3 am.

My husband came home from his fifth and final deployment a different man—and I wasn't the same either. Our daughter was 9 months old, and we all had relearning to do. It was at that time that I got word that my unit would be going back to Afghanistan, and my husband would be stationed in Key West, Florida.

I decided after 13 years of Army Service that I was done. I wasn't coping mentally, and for the first time in my life- I decided to go talk to a therapist because I was dealing with postpartum depression. If I'm being honest, I probably had peripartum depression prior to this, during the pregnancy.

The entire first year of her life was a blur- and I wasn't mentally handling solo parenting. With the three PCSs in three years, lack of sleep, and 75-pound weight gain that wasn't budging, I wasn't okay. I was put on medication, and I felt like a new human- I went back to iStroll- and honestly could kick myself for missing out on all those opportunities to have friendships, but I made the most of my last three months there.

In June of 2016, we relocated to NAS Key West, a surreal shift for an Army family stepping into the world of the Navy. The sunshine was divine, the people were amazing, and I jumped into spouse life with both feet.

The naval protocol regarding rank fraternization was stringent, separating officers and enlisted to the extent of distinct bases. I learned that quickly and my first coffee- but I did pull a card from my old book and kept a bit of who we were and what my husband did- at bay- and just focused on making impacts. (honestly, thank goodness for medication and sunshine! It makes a world of difference).

It was the first time in my life since I was 17 that I was free. I had no contract, no obligation, and no requirement to anyone. I could do whatever I wanted. My crafty, thrifty, and fitness spark had ignited, and I started two businesses in Key West—an embroidery business and a franchise for an iStroll.

I noticed there were a lot of questions happening in the local Facebook group- but not a lot of people were answering them- or people didn't know the answer. I did, so I started to answer those questions, and connect people with others who might know.

I then found that many local moms didn't know any military families, even though it was only a 4-mile by 6-mile island—insane, I thought—someone could live on this island their entire life and not encounter a military family ever.

I felt like I could have a purpose by connecting others and bringing people together—no official invite or title needed. Leave your spouse's rank and your past life at the door—and of course, kids are welcome!

It was invigorating to feel purpose again- even if it was a self-fabricated purpose. I never wanted to people to feel that dark depression I felt, and I never wanted to miss out again on an opportunity because I didn't feel invited. Something about feeling left out from childhood still triggers me sometimes to this day- but I work very hard to make sure others never feel that way- it is the worst feeling, and I never want anyone ever to feel like they aren't valued or appreciated.

I once saw a quote that said- "be the change you wish to see in the world"- and I really loved that, but then I changed it a bit. I challenge you to be the friend you needed when you started this crazy military journey.

NAS Key West was a dream duty station- and literally the best two years of our Military Journey. When something is that good- I often felt guilty for sharing my sunshine pictures every day on social media- but man I wish I would have so I could get those amazing reminders on Facebook.

We moved to the DC area after Key West, and it rained for what felt like six months; when we got there- we often said it was our tears of sadness for having to leave such a beautiful place.

I'll never forget something telling me to go meet & be friendly with a mom in a park on one of those " I just got here, I have no friends my kids are this age posts". I really did NOT want to go- the last thing I wanted to do was make new friends- I was still morning the loss of the best community I had ever had, as was she- and let me tell you- that one encounter, although it did not flourish into a budding bestie friendship- did make me over 40k, in embroidery referral sales.

Now, I'm not saying go meet with every stranger you meet on the internet in a park- but I am saying- if you're in a slump- here are the things that work for me. Do things that push you outside of your comfort zone, put yourself is rooms you don't feel you belong. Show up when you don't feel like it- and make it about helping others.

We are not meant to be alone—we are not meant to do it solo—and just because you can does not mean you should. Hire the dang house cleaner, a meal delivery service, find a babysitter, or find a group of people you can work out couple of times a month, get a with your baby.

You deserve to be happy, and if all of that fails- (or even before you), try all of that and go talk to someone! I have been happily medicated since 2015, and let me tell you- it has saved my life and my marriage.

This life is not easy- and there are mean people out there, but there are so many amazing spouses out there, too; I hope you find the courage after reading this to try again. To go to the award coffee or the meet the weird girl at bunko, and see if they might be able to introduce you to your next BFF.

If you think this only works in the military world, you're wrong. We recently moved to our forever town- and my husband retires next month, and the local library does a summer reading initiative. They give the families purple yard signs, and they do prize drop-bys if you have the purple yard sign displayed.

We had lived in our neighborhood for about three weeks, and I scoped out my neighborhood- for all the kids- we were coming home from a yard sale (old habits die hard), and I spotted the house. I had been stalking all month long and was having a lemonade stand- now, I'm not really a lemonade fan, but you better believe I whipped around so fast and got out and saw a girl about my daughter's age and a son about my son's age.

I asked the mom- who was in workout clothes, "hey do you work out, or do you just like workout clothes- either way is totally fine, I'm just looking for a local gym to work out"totally awkward- and we still laugh about this to this day. I told them we just moved in, and we had a pool, we liked to drink beer, and we'd love them to come over. Our kids literally hang out nearly every single day- nearly three years later.

So, if you're reading this, this is your sign to do the dang thing. Step out of your comfort zone and be the friend you needed when you started this military journey. If you're at the beginning of your journey, say "yes", and don't be afraid to try new things!

You've got this, and if you'd like to connect, reach out to me at @mrssaracopp on Instagram. I'd love to hear your story and learn more about you!!!

Chapter Four

Unleash Your Inner Warrior Within-Yes, you too- Krystalore Crews

Hey there, incredible military spouses! Buckle up because we're about to dive into a rollercoaster of self-discovery, resilience, and a whole lot of love – all served with a side of Crews Beyond Limits flair!

So, picture this: the long-awaited email drops into your inbox, military orders to a new adventure. Excitement bubbles up, but beneath the surface, a wave of emotions is doing the cha-cha. Leaving your comfort zone – your cherished hometown – feels like saying goodbye to a piece of your identity. Buffalo, you've been the peanut butter to my jelly, the mac to my cheese, and leaving you? Well, that's like leaving behind a part of my heart.

But here's the plot twist – we military spouses are pros at turning excitement into tangible action, right? So, there we were, my husband and I, facing the dilemma of sticking to the familiar or embracing the unknown. And guess what? We chose the path less traveled – ending my military career early and tossing ourselves into the whirlwind of change.

Now, Harrisburg, with its quirks and surprises, became our new canvas. The job market wasn't exactly rolling out the red carpet, though. Sound familiar? Rejections and biased comments during interviews had me questioning my worth. I found myself doing the job-search tango, compromising standards, and squeezing myself into molds that didn't quite fit.

And let's not forget the struggles of making friends in a new town – cliques, cliques everywhere! The "What do you do?" question became my arch-nemesis, a reminder of my identity crisis. But hold on, my friends, because here comes the hero of our story – Team Red, White, and Blue! Running with the American flag turned the city into a playground of resilience and connection.

But life's journey isn't all sunshine and rainbows, right? Moves and remote jobs kept me in a perpetual state of "where's home again?" The pursuit of a full-time job felt like a never-ending quest, and I found myself settling for part-time positions in hospitals. Cue the LinkedIn message that sparked hope – "I want to help the next five transitioning Veterans find their purpose after their service." Enter my mentor, Treasa, and a deep dive into entrepreneurship.

Starting a business from scratch, dealing with loneliness and financial strains – it was like riding a unicorn through a storm. Remote work became my sidekick, offering a slice of normalcy in the chaos of military life. And guess what? Pittsburgh beckoned with another move, but this time, armed with resilience, a remote job, and a sprinkle of magic, I thrived in building a national program and global brand of what is now Crews Beyond Limits Consulting, empowering incredible warriors like you to put themselves and their health first for just 34 minutes per day to reduce the stress and overwhelm of life, embrace chaos, and live a more fulfilling life.

Now, the journey wasn't all sunshine and rainbows. Friendships strained, connections crumbled, and there was a fair share of "seriously, you're doing what?" from folks who just didn't get it. But guess what, amazing people? Embracing change became my superpower. I outgrew relationships that didn't serve my growth, found solace in true friendships, and learned that it's okay to curate your tribe.

And here's the magic potion, my fellow warriors – Five Tips for Resilience in Seasons of Change:

1. Know Who You Are to the Core: Picture your core values and personality like the sprinkles on your favorite ice cream – they make life a whole lot sweeter. Embrace the unique sauce that makes you, well, you. Knowing who you are becomes your superhero cape in the face of the crazy twists and turns.

2. Confidence in Posture and Energy by Setting Goals: Let's talk about confidence – it's not just about striking a superhero pose (though that's fun too). It's about setting goals that light your soul on fire. Goals become your trusty sidekick, guiding you through the stormy seas of change. And trust me, confidence isn't just about how you look; it's about radiating that inner sparkle when you're in sync with your purpose.

3. Consistency in Pursuit of Goals with a Healthy Lifestyle: Resilience? It's not born in a day; it's forged in the fire of consistency. Once you've set those fantastic goals, stay consistent. Think of it like building a sandcastle – each grain of consistency shapes your masterpiece. And oh, don't forget the healthy lifestyle vibes; they're the

secret sauce to mental resilience, giving you the strength to face any challenge. Consider tracking your progress by using my free habit tracker www.krystalorecrews.com/habittracker.

4.Community and Powerful Connections: Forget the small talk; let's talk powerful connections. Build a community that's not just a bunch of faces; it's your anchor in the crazy tides of military life. Surround yourself with fellow warriors who get the journey. Powerful connections? They're like having a squad of superheroes cheering you on when the going gets tough. Still struggling to find your tribe? Consider joining my virtual tribe with incredible warrior spouses all over the world. https://www.facebook.com/groups/crewsbeyondlimits

5.Daily Celebration of All Wins Big and Small, and Gratitude: Imagine your journey as a series of victories, big and small, each one a stepping stone to your superhero status. Celebrate them all – the big triumphs and the tiny victories. Cultivate a daily dose of gratitude; it's like a magic wand turning ordinary moments into extraordinary blessings.

As the pages of your superhero origin story unfold, remember – the warrior within you is emerging stronger, more resilient, and ready to face any chapter with courage and tenacity. Seasons of change? They're not your adversaries; they're your dance partners in the grand ball of self-discovery and untapped potential.

And here's the deal, my awesome friends – don't wait until it's too late to know who you are without your spouse. Put yourself and your health first, always. You're not just a supporting character in this epic adventure; you're the lead, the hero, the star of your own show.

Yes, you're worthy of the light and love too, my friend.

So, go on, dance in the rain, laugh with all your heart, and take that leap into the unknown. The warrior within? It's you, and the world is waiting for your unique magic. Until next time, keep shining, keep exploring, and keep being the incredible warrior that you are!

Crews Beyond Limits Journal Prompts:

1. Reflect on the role of teamwork in your own life. How can you actively cultivate an environment of mutual assistance and encouragement within your relationships?

2. Imagine you've hired a coach to guide you through your current challenges. What specific areas would you want to focus on with your coach? How do you envision their support helping you navigate this phase of your life?

3. Reflect on your journey of change and evolving identity. How has your commitment to fitness and wellness impacted your resilience? Imagine writing a letter to your present self from a future version who emerged even stronger from this transformation.

Remember, you've got this, and your journey is a masterpiece in the making too-if you say yes to YOU!

Chapter Five

Don't Be A Dependa- Sienna Newton Dohse

In this chapter, you will get a small glimpse into the chaotic world of a military spouse. It is meant to be light-hearted and funny but also to address common occurrences. Please don't read this feeling personally attacked, but rather be more aware of the potential perceptions should you find yourself in one of these is a compilation of stories and instances from both new and old military spouse situations. These are mostly women; the men I spoke with about their experiences sang a different tune.

Each branch of service has its fair share of issues associated with their communities. So, you've entered the world of military life as a newly hitched bride or groom, and there's a lot to navigate! Let's dive deep into some valuable insights on how not to be a "dependa" and maintain a positive military spouse experience. As a woman, spouse, and military leader, I've gathered a mix of do's and don'ts from various perspectives, aiming for a balanced approach.

With information at our fingertips, you can find anything and everything on social media. Scrolling through endless posts, you've likely seen or heard the term "dependa" associated with a not-so-flattering viral post of a military spouse. It is sometimes in jest, sometimes not. As someone with over 20 years of service, I've had my share of conversations with fellow military spouses, co-workers, and other service members.

This chapter explores how to avoid falling into the "dependa" stereotype – a term that, depending on context, can be either nonchalant banter or hurt feelings. "You had me at Tri-Care", "BAH bae" and "our rank" are just a few of the comments to avoid.

Definition and Origins of Dependa: de·pen·da

: one that is [dependent](#) on a military service member

A "dependa" is the "Karen" of military spouses.

(except civilian-spouse Karens don't expect you to salute them).

"The term is a military community slur, a socially acceptable word to demean military spouses who utilize the benefits afforded to their active-duty service members. According to social media portrayals, a dependa "wears rank" and adopts and embraces the two-for-one mentality that many of us try to shake.

They are senior military spouses, mostly wives, who whisper, "I've earned this" to themselves before they demand service on base." – military.com

Having a solid understanding of Emotional Intelligence (ie. Self-awareness, self- management, social awareness and relationship management) will help you avoid falling into the pitfalls of military spouse stereotypes. This also requires empathy and resilience. It's important to remember that stereotypes don't define individuals and to resist the urge to engage in online arguments on social media unit spouse's page or demeaning behavior towards the employees at the Base Exchange. You could easily secure your spouse a trip the Chief's office for a very uncomfortable conversation.

Understanding the military lifestyle can be fun and exciting, or it can be stepping out of your comfort zone. Either way, it comes with its own set of challenges; it's up to you if you're ready to face them with an open mindset.

We all have our own reasons for joining the military. For many, this stems from a sense of duty, purpose, patriotism, or a desire for adventure. Some of us were raised in military families or those affected by events like 9/11, which can inspire a deep sense of national pride and a desire to protect one's country.

Once in the military, it becomes more than just a job; it's a lifestyle characterized by discipline, sacrifice, and camaraderie. Understanding the unique challenges and demands of military life is essential for both service members and their spouses. It involves adapting to frequent moves, deployments, long hours, and the constant possibility of danger.

Stay informed about military life and its challenges so you can better understand and support your partner. Establish healthy boundaries to maintain a balance between personal space and shared military activities within the relationship. Despite these challenges, many find fulfillment and a strong sense of belonging in the military community.

A navy friend of mine recently commented about an event she attended with her husband. Another spouse was the talk of the event because of her inappropriate attire. How can this be avoided? I'm not telling you how to dress, nor am I some high-end fashionista. I'm just sharing some suggestions and recommendations and a brief description of the different social gatherings.

For military ceremonies like a change of command, promotion, or retirement ceremony, it's crucial to dress in appropriate attire that reflects the significance of the occasion and shows respect for your service member and their uniform. You do not want to be the one being gawked at or have their picture shared on the other spouse's group chats. "Opting for key, essential business or dressy casual outfits is a good choice (simple black dress or dress slacks and blouse with low heel), ensuring that the attire is both respectful and formal," says a Navy spouse.

It's essential to be mindful of your spouse's uniform and dress accordingly, choosing attire that complements it without overshadowing it. Aim for a classy and sophisticated look, avoiding anything too revealing or inappropriate for the seriousness of the event. Funerals, no matter military or civilian, is a no-brainer in how one should dress, but have respect for yourself and everyone attending. Ultimately, dressing in a manner that honors the occasion and shows respect for your spouse's service and achievements is highly recommended and suggested.

Fitness and self-care are always a plus in having a healthy lifestyle and are highly encouraged! Let's be real; most of us grab a pair of leggings, a t-shirt, or a hoodie, throw our hair in a bun, and hit the gym. Then there are the others who put much more effort into their gym attire but might not be appropriate for the base gym.

Military spouses need to do so with respect for gym rules and regulations. Notice the signs posted all over the locker room and weight room. Spending time selecting workout attire is understandable, but it's important to adhere to the dress code posted in the gym. Wearing small sports bras or extremely short shorts that violate rules not only draws negative attention but also undermines the professionalism and respect expected in a military environment. It's essential to recognize and abide by the signs posted regarding appropriate attire. "Attempting to use your spouse's rank or status to bend the rules is inappropriate and unlikely to be effective; I don't care who your spouse is. Put more clothes on, please." Showing respect for gym staff and fellow gym-goers by adhering to the guidelines fosters a positive, safe, and comfortable environment for all.

Telling the gym employee you will not change clothes or leave or better yet, asking them, "Do you know who your lieutenant pilot husband is?" will not get you very far when the Command Sergeant Major of the Marine Corps unit on base is standing right there at the counter supporting the gym staff, telling you to leave to protect you and his Marines. I promise you, your lieutenant husband would not appreciate that.

Every now and then, "dependas" have been spotted wearing their spouse's physical training (PT) uniform to the Commissary or to the Base Exchange. This is never okay unless you're in the same branch and you're actually performing PT.

Communication in relationships is key to a loving and long-lasting union. It is even more effective when it comes to being in a military family with a lot of moving parts and pieces. Your spouse will more than likely have orders to Permanent Change of Station, also known PCS. Pack your things; you're moving;! Unless they get unaccompanied orders, but that should be another book in its entirety. As the spouse, be supportive and helpful. Foster open communication with your partner, ensuring both of you are aware of each other's expectations and responsibilities during the move. How can you help? Engage! Go to the PCS briefings.

"My husband got orders to Japan, and we had three months to get ready. He was working long days and I was a full-time student. Recently separated from the military, I understood the stress my husband was under, so I took on the challenges of getting us packed up and ready for the movers. Taking this off his plate was such a relief, but we're a team working together.

We went to our out-processing briefing, where the lady walked us through the process step by step. Logging onto our account and scheduling the movers was simple. I was able to knock out homework before and after the movers came to pack up our things. Reassuring my husband throughout this PCS brought us closer together, and we were able to enjoy our time while stationed in Japan."

This was a success story. There are more horrifying examples of what the elusive "dependa" says and does during this daunting moment in one's military career. "We're moving where!?! Away from my friends and family?? Ew, what kind of food do they have there? I don't know anyone over there..." The list goes on and on. Discuss the concerns with your spouse; this is their career, with little to no control over where they are stationed. This is what you signed up for when marrying someone in the military.

Temporary duty or TDYs and deployments aren't as tough and are easier to manage. Know the why! Why are they going there? What are they doing day to day? What is the purpose of the mission? Know these things within reason and the understanding that this is THEIR JOB.

TDYs and deployments come with irregular work hours; this isn't a nine-to-five type of job to begin with, and it is even worse when they're on the other side of the world. Managing your expectations of not knowing when they will have cell service, Wi-Fi, or any form of communication immediately will better prepare you mentally and emotionally. Talk about it and understand the situation. Put yourself in their shoes. "When we were able to call home, I liked to hear about what she's doing, how my kids are doing… the normal everyday stuff back home is what helps me escape momentarily," said an Army buddy of mine.

The service member may not want to talk about work, however that may not reflect something negative, just simply not able to talk about it. Complaining about the water heater or mom drama at school makes for a very short conversation, or worse; it can cause more stress because they aren't home to help or fix the issues. Roll up your sleeves and get to work! Take care of the household issues while they're gone. Stressors of the job may lead to delayed communication or emotional reactions for the service member. This requires the application and knowledge of emotional intelligence.

"Stay present in the now, keep busy," said a Marine Corps brother. "Nothing else matters, it makes the transition in and out easier and networking. Don't take things personal when they bring home their work. I try to stay involved with family and children, getting to know her co-workers and their spouses."

During deployments, my friend said that the spouses would help each other. "I would do stuff for the clinic, organize and cook for pot-luck lunches; I try to be helpful. We would seek out the newer spouses and help them connect with resources and others who may be of assistance." Connections or building friendships and knowing who to go to can be helpful when you can't reach your spouse; they might have information you missed out on.

While your loved one is deployed, DO NOT POST DETAILS ON SOCIAL MEDIA. Read that sentence again if you need to. Operations Security or OPSEC and social media do not mix, ever. You will learn the details about this topic when the time comes. For now, just know not to do it. Don't be the "dependa" on the World Wide Web posting troop movement day to day. That can easily get your spouse in serious trouble, cause a delay in their homecoming, or worse, have them killed.

While we're on the subject of social media, don't be a jerk! Spouse groups are meant to be helpful and supportive. You will find a lot of people on there with the same questions or concerns. However, some can be toxic and vicious. Do not engage.

"Don't fight your spouse's battles for them... especially on social media. They have a chain of command for a reason. Keep unhappy marriage issues at home... the entire unit/base does not need to know; that's what the chaplain and marriage counselors are for," said an Air Force friend of mine.

"I'm in the same unit as my husband, between the two of us, we can figure out who the anonymous poster is on the base spouse page. Your spouse aka "your sponsor" (unless dual mil) is responsible for everything you do and don't do; i.e. speeding tickets, shoplifting, inappropriate attire on base, etc. Keep your house clean and food on the table."

Finding a supportive online community or joining a group to do an activity to get you out of the house are healthier ways to build relationships with others who are experiencing the same struggles you may have. Volunteering with local non-profit organizations outside the military bubble can also foster positive connections with neighbors while contributing to the local community. You might find out who the "go-to" plumber is to fix that pesky water heater that's giving you problems.

"Keep or find civilian friends! When it comes to making friends, consider this golden rule: Only make friends with locals. Avoid the drama-prone base acquaintances and steer clear of gossip," said a Navy spouse of 30 years. "Living on base can feel like a daily obstacle course, especially in places like Sigonella and Guam. And a tip from the trenches – be cautious around team and pilot wives; some may dub them the true "Karen's of military spouses." Demanding.

They were Karen's before Karen's were cool," she said laughingly. I personally have never encountered this situation and had positive relationships with various groups of wives from all branches of service. Again, each of us will have different experiences, the only thing that matters is which category do you fall in?

That leads us right to the subject of the "Do You Know Who My Husband Is?" syndrome. A "dependa's" infamous "Do you know who my husband is" line is a quick way to earn an eye-roll. Avoid saying this at all cost, especially when it comes to expedited favors at the exchange or asking for a military discount. Remember, your spouse's rank is just that – your spouse's. Be proud, supportive, and encouraging, but don't let it overshadow their service and sacrifice. Don't expect to be saluted at the front gate or any other time.

"Circa 1990 something… It was 10 hours into my 8-hour day, and I was standing gate duty; this one woman got so pissed at me because I didn't salute her. "Don't you see the blue base sticker…" she asked. "Yes, ma'am, but I don't salute a sticker, but the officer with the ID." She got so mad, that she pulled over, went into the security office, and raised some serious hell. Security came and got her… she was cuffed in the back of the security car, and of course, I rendered a proper salute as she was carted off.

– Anonymous

The sense of entitlement because of "who their spouse is" was almost a unanimous comment in my little survey. It's essential to recognize and appreciate the sacrifices made by your service member and to understand that military benefits are earned through their service.

Additionally, actively participating in the military community, volunteering, and supporting fellow spouses can help foster a sense of unity and shared responsibility rather than entitlement. This can also build better relationships between enlisted and officer spouses. One is not better or more important than the other, but maintaining open communication with each other and being mindful of the challenges they face can also help prevent entitlement attitudes from developing.

"We would laugh at each other when we would see the commander's wife park in the parking spot reserved for a colonel." – Army MP

Overall, focusing on empathy (there's that word again!), humility, and contributing positively to the community can help you as a military spouse avoid entitlement and privilege attitudes. "The military member earned their rank and achieved their goals to get where they are." Some spouses play a huge part in that, but that doesn't give them the right to certain base entitlements and benefits. "Instead, they should focus on their own personal development." Pursuing higher education and accomplishing career goals will benefit you in the long run and set you apart from the rest.

Taking advantage of the education benefits for military spouses is one of the best things we have offered to us! Online classes and on base, I'm sure you will find something that interests you! Invest time in developing your skills and pursuing personal growth to contribute meaningfully to your relationship. Cultivating your own interests and friendships, maintaining a sense of individuality outside of the military circle will keep you out of the negative spotlight.

This will help with balancing your own interests and not get you roped into the dance mom or little league baseball drama. Being the spouse who is drama free, independent and confident in themselves is a great way of not earning the dreadful "dependa" title.

"While you're shopping at the base exchange for the basic necessities, you run into Becky, who is sporting her new Louis Vuitton purse. As a newlywed to an E-3 barely making ends meet, do not go and buy that Gucci purse on display!"

Financial responsibility and keeping up with the Joneses is never a fun topic of discussion, but it happens! If your lower- ranking husband has to choose between a haircut to keep him in uniform standards or to fill the gas tank so he can get to work, ask yourself, "do you really need that purse? Do you really need to go out day drinking with your college girlfriends?" The answer is no!

Put the purse down and walk away. The importance of financial literacy and knowing how to read an LES, a leave and earnings statement, will help you budget your monthly costs. Categorize your needs and wants: you NEED food, baby wipes, and cleaning supplies. You don't need the new gaming system or a Coach purse.

Based off of experiences of senior leaders, hearing and witnessing terrible situations our junior service members faced, those material things should not come before the needs of human life or a financial crisis.

"You don't want to be the "depenced" walking around with a high-end name-brand purse while dragging your raggedy, dirty snot-nosed babies around the store. Then you have your landlord call your husband's command complaining you haven't paid rent in months and your electricity is about to be cut off."

Women aren't the only ones with a spending problem. "We had a young sailor who became an avid gun collector at his first duty station, which is fine. The problem was he wasn't paying the bills. They were behind on their rent, credit cards were maxed out, and they didn't have money for gas. He kept borrowing money from people at work for gas. That's when we started finding out about their financial issues."

If you enjoy shopping or have an expensive hobby, maybe have a part-time job to offset the cost of the "wants" to avoid going without the "needs." If you're talented or crafty, spouses can apply for a Home Base Business license to make a little extra spending cash. Actively contribute to shared responsibilities, whether it's household chores, planning, or financial decision-making. Strive to manage your finances responsibly and avoid relying solely on others for financial support. Once leadership is involved, it is no longer a private matter. There are financial counselors available on base for assistance to educate you or to get you back on track.

You and your spouse are now settled in to his or her new command. For my female spouses, consider this for perspective; this is just generalization: there are more women serving in the military today than in decades past. According to the DOD annual demographics report, "in 2021 women made up 17.3% of the active duty force, totaling 231,741 members." The numbers still show that the military is a male-dominated career field. Which means your husband may have a female or two in his unit. Does this mean you should be concerned? No, because your spouse is not everyone's cup of tea.

"I love hearing or reading news that I'm trying to steal my co-worker from his wife; that always makes things fun at work," said a female Army friend of mine stationed on the West Coast. "Here's my advice on that... not every woman your husband works with wants him and vice versa; get to know everyone at the unit first."

Another topic relevant to this chapter is that not everyone wants your spouse. It's crucial not to make assumptions about others' relationships based on unfounded suspicions. Most military units are close-knit teams that need to rely on each other and communicate in ways some do not understand. If you and your spouse have a history of infidelity or other issues, then this could be a factor.

Recognizing your own insecurities and communicating concerns with your spouse can help with these issues that could potentially hurt your marriage. Communication outside of work will happen for the service member; it's a 24/7 job. On the other hand, I would personally try to keep work comms to a minimum. Texting or calling past 7p.m. would mean a response is needed for the next work day.

"One day I was contacted by a local non-profit organization that was hosting a celebrity golf tournament. They signed on two more celebrities therefore they needed a few more military golfers. So I called and texted every golfer I had in my contacts. It was after 7p.m. and they needed names ASAP. About 45 minutes later I get a phone call from a number I did not recognize. Thinking it was another person from the golf tournament, I answered immediately, Hello, can I help you? I was greeted on the other end of the line by a very upset woman yelling and screaming at me. "Who the hell are you calling my husband after hours?"

I calmly sat there and listened to her rant; when she finally came up for air, I simply asked "Ma'am, which one is your husband, because I contacted between 35 and 40 golfers." There was a brief pause….. no answer….. "Please note that I will never contact your husband for another community relations event, thank you, and have a good evening." Then I hung up before she could get another word in to further embarrass her husband.

The next day, the Gunny called me, apologizing for his wife's behavior and thanked me for the invite and tried to explain the situation. I was able to stop him, since their issues are none of my business but understood enough to end the conversation."

The other part of that story was the spouses were encouraged to participate; they needed help with the ditty bags, prizes, and the little here-and-there details. Try to be understanding and supportive. This was an example of two people who didn't work together day to day, but in a joint forces environment, they are peers. Daily interactions creates a network from each of the different commands on base.

I'll wrap this up with a few "do's and don'ts" to help you move forward in your role as a military spouse:

1. Excessive Complaints: Constantly complaining about military life without seeking solutions or adapting to the challenges can be draining.

2. Unrealistic Expectations: Having unrealistic expectations about the military lifestyle or demanding special treatment can strain relationships. Be emotionally supportive to your partner and seek support when needed, fostering a strong and resilient connection.

3. Oversharing Personal Drama: Sharing overly personal or dramatic details about your relationship issues can make others uncomfortable.

4. Constant Comparisons: Continuously comparing your partner's military experience to others can create unnecessary tension and dissatisfaction.

5. Overreliance on Benefits: Relying solely on military benefits without actively contributing to the relationship or household can be perceived as entitlement.

6. Ignoring Opinions: Dismissing others' perspectives or advice, especially from experienced military spouses, may hinder personal growth and adaptation.

7. Gossiping: Engaging in gossip or spreading rumors within military communities can harm relationships and create a negative environment.

8. Victim Mentality: Adopting a victim mentality without taking responsibility for personal actions can strain relationships and hinder personal development. Regularly reflect on your actions and behaviors

to ensure you are not relying excessively on others and are actively contributing to the relationship.

9. Demanding Special Treatment: Expecting special treatment or privileges due to your partner's military service may lead to resentment from others.

10. Lack of Independence: Failing to maintain personal independence and solely relying on your partner for emotional or financial support can be burdensome and unhealthy. Pursue your own career goals and ambitions, contributing to a sense of fulfillment and reducing dependency.

In summary, embrace your role as a military spouse with pride, steer clear of drama, resist the urge to gossip, and maintain humility in all situations. By following these guidelines, you'll navigate military life with grace. Contribute positively to your community and make it through the 20+ years of your spouse's career not being called "the dependa."

Chapter Six

Transition To Transformation-Michelle Faust

The brisk mid-December wind blows at my back as the sound of a car door rings out behind me. The dress and shoes that I am wearing are little help against the cold. Quick, short steps lead me to the door; warmth and comfort are a welcome greeting. Quickly looking around, I see where my fiance and I are supposed to go.

This was not what I imagined for this day. Most girls dream of a massive wedding in a church surrounded by family and friends, with flowers, cake, and a reception. This was lightyears away from anything I had imagined. It was just us, the justice of peace, and two friends I did not know very well.

From the moment the justice of the peace said, "I pronounce you Mr. and Mrs. Faust," I transitioned into a military spouse. Growing up in Seattle, WA, I was completely unaware that I lived close to various military bases. No one in my family served in the military, and in the community of people I lived in, I did not know anyone who served in the military. They say ignorance is bliss; I was unaware of just how difficult things were about to be.

Early spring news came, which was wonderful and hard at the same time. We had only been married four months, and now we faced two major life events: our first child and first deployment. I knew I was married to an active-duty Air Force man and understood that deployments were part of the deal. He would be gone for four months. Thankfully, my due date was right when he was coming home.

My husband now deployed, I went to connect with the other military spouses at the base and tried to build some friendships. Small talk and surface conversations over the weeks started to build some connections. One day, I felt safe enough to tell someone that I was having a hard time because my husband had left, and I was told I had no right because her husband had gone for 18 months. If I could not handle it, I should have never gotten married.

From that day, I did not feel safe in the group of other military spouses and eventually pulled away. In this group, any sign of weakness was met with disrespect. Air Force officer's wives treated me like a second-class citizen and made it abundantly clear I was not welcome at events. No matter how hard I tried, I was met with rejection. I was already struggling as a newlywed without my husband and a pregnancy; this level of rejection was something I did not need.

I found myself finding comfort day after day alone, texting my husband on Messenger. He had access to a computer most of the day, and it made the days a little easier to cope with. Months passed by marked with loneliness and isolation. Thankfully, our first deployment was only four months. He returned just in time for the birth of our first child.

No one prepared me for the challenges that would come from a spouse returning from a deployment. The added element of having our first child magnified the problems that were underlying. We would go to the hospitality house on post and see two different types of people. People doing so well that they had no outward problems or people enduring long deployments.

I had a woman that I tried to connect with who had a baby at the same time that I did. Hers slept through the night, and she looked polished and rested. My baby had a severe case of colic, and I was barely surviving. Instead of support, I received judgment from the military spouses and that mom. My hardship was blamed on my inability to keep it together. Instead of being supported or embraced, I was pushed away.

This interaction left me with an understanding. If I could not be pulled all together and hide all of my problems, I would have no place in that community. Even after this, I attempted to go to the women's bible study at the chapel. It's called PWOC. After a season of attending, I found it to be a place of surface connection and a place where women tore each other down, often behind each other's backs. I have never been one to embrace drama, but the culture I encountered seemed to thrive off of it.

When I chose to marry into military life, I never accounted that I would take on the role of a military spouse. Instead of just a mother and father-in-law, I also received an entire military spouse family. On this transition I did not take any time to process that I was becoming a military spouse. For some reason, I thought that if I just showed up to events with my husband, everything would go well and be easy. I possibly watched too many romanticized movie scenes featuring well-dressed military wives on colorful furniture, sipping tea, and all having a good time.

The first point I want to share with you is sometimes being a military spouse is hard. You assume that you will automatically fit in with everyone simply because you are a spouse, but this is not true. Do not do what I did, which is pull away, but continue to look for people who will provide support. Just because you encounter drama does not mean there are no genuine people. If you pull away, you will not find those genuine support people. Chances are you are the one who is going to have to look; they are not coming to you.

A few kids later, we again were in transition. My husband had a real heart for helping people, so he decided to cross-train in mental health from communications. The change required my husband to go to a new tech school. While he did well in school, it became clear that this new job was not a good fit. He did well academically but practically did not do well. He had a hard time mentally detaching from situations and disconnecting. Moving from de-escalating a potentially violent person to just going to lunch was mentally impossible for my husband.

This was just the tip of the iceberg of issues that made it clear this change away from his last job was not having a good outcome. The ending of his school came with a deployment. He communicated that he was not ready to go because of the issues, but his leadership ignored him and sent him away anyway. I was left alone with no support, with four kids under five years old.

A few weeks into the deployment, it became clear to the leadership down where my husband was that my husband was not properly prepared. This was no surprise to us because we knew, and my husband tried to communicate this before he left. As a result, they let him know he would be sent back. Before my husband arrived back, I had a conversation with his commander, and I was assured that my husband could go back to communications.

Shortly after returning, the regulation changed, and instead of being allowed back to his past job, he was transitioned straight out of active duty with an honorable discharge. Up until this point, I had trust in my husband's leadership. Now, I felt like that trust had been betrayed. All of the words of assurance from that commander inspire anger and frustration.

This sudden and unplanned change triggered a cycle of near-homelessness. The skills that my husband had been using for twelve years equaled a minimum wage job as a civilian. Our military friends would give well-meaning advice or blatant judgment, asserting that my husband had to be some horrible person for life to be dealing us these cards.

The second point I want to make is that, as a military spouse, the greatest thing you can do is support your spouse. It's easy to stand and clap at different ceremonies and events, but how do you react on the worst day of your spouse's career? The day they lose everything and your financial stability is destroyed? Do you become another voice already shouting at your spouse that they are a failure, or do you truly overlook the storm and be a strong support?

Our greatest days are not defined by platforms of celebration and honor. They are defined by how we navigate our lowest moments. Military spouses are one of the toughest groups of people on the planet, and their resilience is developed in times of hardship.

When we encounter hardship, it is easy to want to attach a time stamp and limit. Are things going to be hard in a week, month or year? Just how long do you go before you throw in the towel and accept that no change is coming? How many times do you get knocked down before it is one too many blows? As a spouse, when do we say I can do better if I just left?

When your life seems like one big storm, and you see your military husband lose it all, these are real questions. I would find myself surrounded by military families who were doing amazing by my standards and feel the gap ever widening. First, it was the fact that I was an Air Force spouse whose struggles were not allowed to be shared because, compared to everyone else, mine did not matter. Now, I was surrounded by families whose husbands could provide well, and I was attached to the only one who seemingly couldn't.

The third point I want to make is that perceptions are dangerous. Military spouses are bred to look the part—perfect makeup, hair, and smiles. Always be polite and always be involved in everything. When everyone is putting up a front that their life is perfect, the one who does not have the energy to do so tends to assume they are the defective one. In reality, under perfect makeup and manners, hardships are hidden. It's too personally dangerous for polished people to risk being exposed to ever being real around people, especially when the goal is to impress and meet a standard continually.

Through this, my husband worked hard in every way he could, and in 2013, things started looking up for us. We just moved to Washington State, and my husband finally landed a good government contract. His job took him to different naval bases to do computer work. We were stable enough to rent a house and start attacking the financial damage near homelessness created.

During this season, my husband made a connection and was thankfully allowed back into the Air Force reserves. September 16th, 2013, is a day I will never forget. He had drilled locally, so he was redirected from the worksite that he had been scheduled to go to—the D.C. Navel Yard out on the East Coast.

My husband was working under a desk listening to the TV playing in the background, and they announced a shooting that had just taken place. Over the course of time, it was revealed that the company the shooter worked for matched what was on my husband's badge. More time revealed the shooter that ended the lives of 13 people was his direct coworker. Had he been in DC that day, there is a high chance I would have lost my husband.

We got thrown back into instability because the government's solution to the problem was eliminating every contract, including my husband's. Here, we just rented a house, and now we were suddenly and forcefully unemployed again. The cycle we thought we broke, though frustratingly, continued. When we met with people from the military and church, most of them cast judgment. Blaming my husband fully, as if there was an assumption that he single-handedly caused the shooter to do what he did and purposefully caused the contracts for everyone to disappear.

The fourth thing I want to share is as a military spouse; we must not listen to what everyone is saying to us. It is easy for anyone to cast judgment or assert their strong opinion. Just because everyone is agreeing does not mean it is automatically true. Sometimes it's best to choose to listen to the people closest to you, and in this case, it was my husband. The people who were the most unsupportive and harsh tended to be the ones who had the least amount of effort or support for my family.

If you encounter a military family going through hard times, think before you criticize. Take even more time before you use words to harshly judge someone. Stating you disagree with someone and forcing your disapproval on a really hurting person and family does nothing but harm. If you find yourself unable to be kind, then the best thing you can do for that family is simply leave them alone and say nothing. It does not take someone pointing out what a family already knows and is trying desperately to correct already.

Another move to a new base. I loved this new state because it was warm. I was super involved in church, and my husband was between working his job and being an Air Force reservist. Life, for a moment, seemed normal and stable, yet again, life does not always play fair.

I am in the middle of my morning caring for my kids when my phone rings. My husband usually calls me on his way to work to talk, but this conversation was different from most. He told me his back was hurting severely and that he was unsure if he would even be able to get out of the car when he arrived at work.

That phone call ended, and shortly after, I received another call. My husband had attempted to get out of the car but discovered he was unable to walk due to a disk in his back that slipped. He ended up army crawling in the parking lot until someone found him, and he got loaded into an ambulance and taken to the hospital.

The people from the church I attended went to visit and, instead of support, used that time to communicate that my husband was a bad provider and this was his fault. That he should abandon the military and recreate himself. The women looked at me with disgust because I continued to support my husband. Everyone was expecting me to say enough was enough and file divorce papers.

My husband came home and needed a walker. It took him the better part of nine months to regain his ability to walk again. Thoughts of all of the trials we had been through, and now this. Truly, life has no limit to how hard things may become.

The difference between defeat and victory is the choice to get back up that one final time. The thing is, we don't know when that final time is; we cannot see it in real time. If we quit, we will never know how close we were to breakthrough. The time stamp that our lives had for near homelessness and trials was ten years. All the way from 2009 to 2019. In the middle of this time frame, hit after hit came, and my husband just kept getting back up. He did not always get back up because he understood that things would be better, but he refused to quit.

The fifth point I want to make is hard times are what push you to understand your why. Your struggle is what briths the passion that you have, and creates the drive that moves you forward. How many people go through horrible circumstance only later to champion entire movements against social issues or become solid supporters and icons to those who are now struggling the same way?

My husband and I have a passion for helping the military, veterans, and first responders from the bedroom to the prayer room. Without the years of intense struggles, we would lack the perspective and empathy to truly care and connect with people who have deep needs and are working harder than anyone understands.

As close to homelessness as we have been more than once, I can tell you I don't just jump to conclusions or judgment anymore when I interact with a homeless person. When I see a disconnected and stressed-out young military spouse, I do not attempt to give advice or tell her what she is doing wrong. If I go into the home of a mom who has a husband who is away, I don't tell her or think, how could the house be so messy? What I do now is I choose to listen, be kind, and offer to help in any way I can.

Transition to a military spouse happens much earlier than a transformation into a military spouse. I became a military spouse on my wedding day, but I did not transition into someone walking in empathy, kindness, and person that was walking looking at the needs of others until much later.

Military spouses have a bond that goes across every branch, enduring situations that our civilian friends will never need to. We don't just exist as a husband or wife to our active duty or reserve spouse. We stand as pillars of stability to our families, reaching out to help and support our fellow spouses.

We have a responsibility to leave no military spouse behind. When we overlook those in need around us, this weakens the community, and spouses can suffer alone and enter a state of isolation. When we choose to leave no military spouse behind, we are choosing to strengthen the community as a whole; every military spouse is embraced, supported, and in a strong community.

Understand that being a military spouse is challenging, but lean in any way and look for those who can provide support. Support your spouse not just on the good days of honor but on the day that you lose everything, and encourage your spouse to keep getting back up even when it seems hopeless; victory only comes to those who do not quit.

Do not get in the habit of making judgments of other people or looking at other people and comparing situations. Chances are many around you have issues, but they are too polished to ever show it publicly.

Lastly, lean into your struggles and understand your why and passion is hidden in the pain. No, we cannot champion every cause, but we can become a champion for our personal why birthed out of seasons of struggles, and pain.

Over the past seventeen years of being a military spouse, I can truly say our passion and drive come from the depths of the darkest, most hopeless seasons and that is the reason we want to see no military spouse left behind.

Now, you may be asking how I can personally leave no military spouse behind or how I can lean into my own personal struggle to find the victory that I have told you about in this chapter. While I could attempt to give a simple answer to this, every situation is completely unique.

It is nearly impossible for me to fit seventeen years of advice into a five-thousand-word chapter. I want to let you know that my husband and I are available to answer all of your questions.

One of my favorite things to do these days is to sit and listen to someone's story over a cup of coffee or tea. I have also spent many hours on video chat with people pouring out their hearts and situations. Sometimes, I feel led to give advice, and others just listen.

My husband and I are currently doing this to leave no military spouses behind: We are making ourselves available to listen, support, and encourage other military spouses. We also believe in the power of connections and if we know of a resource that can help you, we value providing the guidance.

My husband and I currently have one-on-one meetings, both in person and over the Internet. We are also available for podcasts, interviews, and events, both large and small.

If you are interested in connecting with us please send us an email to:

Agapefamily121806@me.com, or visit www.facebook.com/daniel.faust.33

Also, please check out Daniel Faust's YouTube channel: Warhero2Superhero. Daniel has a passion for uplifting the veteran community and highlighting individuals who are making an impact. We believe that inside of every person who has served our country, there is a superhero inside. My husband's passion is to help someone see that and see that come out to the benefit of the entire veteran community.

https://www.youtube.com/@warhero2superhero

We see so many stories of our veterans encountering homelessness, and dealing with addiction. There is no shortage of visibility on the way veterans struggle. We are actively working to change the narrative, by guiding veterans from transition to transformation.

This chapter focused on the transformation that I personally went through from transitioning to a military spouse to transforming into one. This concept of transition to transformation is not limited to my story. Every single military member in the service goes through a version of this.

Sometimes, the transition to transformation occurs upon entry into the service or when a military veteran exits the service into civilian life. The place my husband and I focus the most is helping navigate the transition from active duty to civilian life. So many times, this process destroys people.

Let me ask you a question. What is causing the homeless among the veteran population in our country? According to https://news.va.gov/126913/veteran-homelessness-increased-by-7-4-in-2023/

"The data showed that on a single night in January 2023, there were 35,574 Veterans who experienced homelessness in the U.S. This reflects a 7.4% increase in the number of Veterans experiencing homelessness from 2022."

According to an article in News Week https://www.newsweek.com/americas-homeless-veteran-problem-getting-worse-1857955

"The number of homeless veterans increased 7.4 percent in the same period, the largest in 12 years. The 35,574 homeless veterans in 2023, equating to 22 of every 10,000 vets, included a 14 percent rise in the number of unsheltered veterans (1,943 more veterans) and a 3 percent increase in veterans experiencing sheltered homelessness (502 more veterans)."

Some assume this boils down to drug addiction, financial irresponsibility, and other poor choices, but I tell you the root issue for so many is they did not transition well. A lack of solid supported transition leads to a failure to transform in a way that leads to a strong community.

This ejection from service into instability is one of the main contributors to the suicide epidemic we are encountering in the veteran community. These men and women exit the service not understanding the challenges ahead. They look for help but find themselves lost in a sea of inadequate services, encountering people who don't understand.

This causes an average of 22 veterans a day to end their lives. In a 30-day month, that is an average of 660 people, and in one year, that number is 7,920 souls lost. My husband and I believe that if we can reach a veteran to help them transition, we can help guide them away from the statistics. The world needs to see more veterans transform into success stories, then an addition to the above numbers.

Together, we all have the power to leave no military spouse behind. We aim to be agents for supporting our veterans through the trials of transition. So here are a few things you can do today to be someone who is an agent of transformation.

1. If you know a veteran, simply give a call and see how they are doing. Let them know they're not alone.

2. Show compassion to those who are brave enough to be open about their personal struggles. There is so much power in just listening and letting a hurting person know that they have been heard.

3. Become aware of the different military bases that may be near you with volunteer opportunities with places like the USO.

If you are interested in joining Daniel or me in the mission to see the veterans go from transition to transformation, we invite you to do so. Together, we can all make a difference.

www.ingramcontent.com/pod-product-compliance
Lightning Source LLC
LaVergne TN
LVHW010410070526
838199LV00065B/5940